FLIPPING
TO WEALTH

Flipping to Wealth

Launching Your Journey to Financial Freedom Through Real Estate

Justin Colby

©2024 All Rights Reserved. No portion of this book may be reproduced, stored in a retrieval system, or transmitted in any form or by any means-electronic, mechanical, photocopy, recording, scanning, or other-except for brief quotations in critical reviews or articles without the prior permission of the author.

Published by Game Changer Publishing

Paperback ISBN: 978-1-964811-23-9
Hardcover ISBN: 978-1-964811-24-6
Digital: ISBN: 978-1-964811-25-3

www.GameChangerPublishing.com

DEDICATION

To the hustlers, those who want more, those who value their time, and those who understand that money can create the experiences of life. This is for the ones who aren't content with just existing and who strive to push the limits.

Read This First

Just to say thank you for buying and reading my book, I've put together a few free bonus gifts. By scanning the QR codes placed throughout this book, you'll gain access to valuable resources and tools we've customized just for you. I'm confident these will assist you on your journey as you turn the pages toward wealth.

Scan The QR Code:

Flipping to Wealth

Launching Your Journey to Financial Freedom Through Real Estate

Justin Colby

www.GameChangerPublishing.com

Foreword

I wholeheartedly recommend Justin Colby's book, *Flipping to Wealth: Launching Your Journey to Financial Freedom Through Real Estate*, to anyone serious about mastering the art of real estate investing. Justin's expertise shines through every page, offering practical insights and strategies that can turn anyone into a successful real estate investor.

Flipping to Wealth is not just another book on real estate; it's a comprehensive guide that combines Justin's years of experience with a systematic approach to flipping properties. Whether you're a seasoned investor or just starting out, Justin's clear explanations and actionable advice provide a roadmap to navigate the complexities of the real estate market with confidence.

What sets this book apart is Justin's ability to break down complex concepts into easy-to-understand principles. From finding the right properties to financing deals and maximizing profits, *Flipping to Wealth* covers it all. Justin doesn't just teach theory; he shares real-world examples and case studies that illustrate his strategies in action.

As someone who has followed Justin Colby's career and teachings for years, I can attest to his integrity and commitment to helping others succeed in real estate investing. His book is a reflection of his dedication to empowering investors with the knowledge and tools they need to thrive in this competitive industry.

Whether you're looking to flip your first property or enhance your existing portfolio, *Flipping to Wealth* is a must-read. Justin Colby's expertise, combined with his passion for teaching, makes this book an invaluable resource that will undoubtedly accelerate your journey to real estate success.

– *Pace Morby*

"It is not the critic who counts; not the man who points out how the strong man stumbles, or where the doer of deeds could have done them better. The credit belongs to the man who is actually in the arena, whose face is marred by dust and sweat and blood; who strives valiantly; who errs, who comes short again and again, because there is no effort without error and shortcoming; but who does actually strive to do the deeds; who knows great enthusiasms, the great devotions; who spends himself in a worthy cause; who at the best knows in the end the triumph of high achievement, and who at the worst, if he fails, at least fails while daring greatly, so that his place shall never be with those cold and timid souls who neither know victory nor defeat."

– Theodore Roosevelt,
"Citizenship in a Republic" speech delivered at
the Sorbonne in Paris on April 23, 1910

Table of Contents

Introduction 1

Chapter 1 – The Crash and the Comeback 9

Chapter 2 – Where to Start 21

Chapter 3 – Finding Your Next Deal 35

Chapter 4 – Deal or No Deal? 45

Chapter 5 – Money Now or Money Later—or Both 51

Chapter 6 – Creative Finance Structure 61

Chapter 7 – The BRRR method 69

Chapter 8 – Raising Private Money Isn't Hard 75

Bonus Chapter – Social Media 81

Conclusion – You Can Do This. I Believe in You 83

Terminology 87

Introduction

"Some people dream of success, while other people get up every morning and make it happen."
– Wayne Huizenga

As I write this, I'm currently in the hospital, gazing at my newborn son. If you're a parent, you know the incredible amount of love and excitement I'm feeling right now. He is our second child, a healthy bundle of joy who has been an excellent sleeper since birth. But as I sit here in amazement, I also feel overwhelmed—not by the responsibility of parenting two children but by the weight of providing for my entire family.

We all know life these days is a lot more expensive than in the '80s when I was born. This little boy alone has cost me somewhere between five and ten thousand dollars in the last three days. (Yes, I have family health insurance, but my portion of the payment is incredibly expensive.) I mean, to support a family of four, it costs a lot of money to live the way they deserve to.

If you're reading this book right now and think, *Well, I don't need to have all the nicest things and the greatest vacations*, we may not be on the same page. You see, I do believe my wife, kids, and I deserve the very best out of life, and—just to be clear—so do you! As a husband and father of two, I see it as *my* obligation to not just support my family financially but to create a legacy. To not just pay the bills but also set up financial security for them forever. It is my obligation to be the "head lion" of my pride. For this reason, I chose real estate as my life's work. It can create riches beyond belief and unimaginable wealth.

I'm a man who always knew there was more to life than what I saw as a child. I don't have one of those stories where I was homeless or starving for food. My childhood was rough because my mother, father, and stepfather were all alcoholics. As a kid, there were times when I would wake up in the backseat of a car in the middle of the night in an alley while my parents were drinking in a bar. I remember coming home from elementary school with friends to find my mom mumbling to herself on the kitchen floor because she was so drunk in the middle of the day. This was hard for me because I was embarrassed by my mom. I always made excuses about why other parents would need to take me home after school or baseball practice, making me an enabler for her.

I have countless stories like this, but one of the worst was when my mother showed up to my basketball game in high school. The coach benched me for not playing great, and during half-time, my mother came back to the locker room, threw her keys against the window, and screamed at my coach to come out and talk to her. The entire team heard her, and I walked out and had to scold my mother in front of everyone. She was obviously incredibly drunk, and I had to yell at her to go home. That memory takes an emotional toll on me even now while writing this book.

I can tell you endless similar stories, but this book isn't about my childhood. I also want the reader to know that my mother loved me very much; she just had a tough internal battle going on, and she used alcohol to cope with it. I am not really clear on what she was battling, but I was aware that she was diagnosed with bipolar disorder.

Growing up in a stressful environment really shaped me as a kid. I knew I couldn't depend on my parents, which made me grow up really fast. It also made me rely more on my friends. We became really close; we would hang out every day and every weekend. They were my support system without even knowing it. Maybe their parents knew it, but my friends didn't. To this very day, I'm incredibly grateful for the group of friends I had while growing up. It shaped me in a way that they didn't even know.

For example, for one reason or another, most of my closest friends went on to go to impressive colleges such as Brown, Harvard, Stanford, CAL, and UCLA. Well, I didn't have grades like that coming out of high school. I only had a 2.8 grade point average, but I knew I didn't want to be the "stupid" friend, so I went to a junior college and worked my ass off. I ended up with a 3.8 GPA and was accepted to UCLA. I chose UCLA because I had a handful of friends who were already there, and it was in Los Angeles. I wanted to get far away from where I was raised.

Now, I have a funny story about UCLA. I busted my butt there to get good grades, just like I did in junior college. It was a lot. UCLA is a tough school, and you can't just do the minimum, or you will fail. Well, by the time I was set to graduate, I was exhausted. I had one more final paper to write, as I was an English major. These finals were over fifteen-page papers, and I was so tired that I was over it. I convinced myself that my final paper wasn't a big deal since I had done so well in all my other classes and finals. So, I decided to take the easy route, and I plagiarized the entire paper. I mean, out of the fifteen pages, I wrote maybe two paragraphs. I went to the library to copy pages of books, and I used Google to get the rest.

That summer, I was traveling through Europe on a travel abroad program offered by UCLA. While in Spain, I got an email from the Dean. He asked that I call him at once. My heart sank into my stomach as I knew they'd figured out what I had done. I called immediately, and I heard the bad news. I had been caught and would receive an F in the class. Here I was—someone who was so proud to have achieved something no one would have thought possible by graduating from UCLA, but I wasn't able to (yet). I tried to take the easy route and look where it got me. This will be a theme you will see in the book: *Don't skimp, don't look for the easy route, do the hard work, and it will pay off.*

My childhood shaped my success in business in the weirdest of ways. I found that I'd become a people pleaser. I had been so desperate to please my mom in the hope that she wouldn't drink, and I internalized this trait and became likable to everyone. I was also blessed to have such great friends, who—just by them being themselves— pushed me to be better, which got me into one of the most reputable universities in the world. By accomplishing that, I realized I could do anything.

Although my childhood wasn't perfect, my family loved me with everything they had. We lived a meager life, but I never went without, and I always had enough. As I grew up, I realized there was more to life than what I experienced as a child. As a husband and father, I realized the only important thing is spending time with family, and money gives me the ability to have more quality time. So, with that in mind, I have built a business in real estate and created a life that helps me do just that.

Having enough money to do anything I wanted always appealed to me while I was growing up. (I'm forty-two years old as I write this.) I wanted to go on more vacations, have a bigger house, and drive nicer cars. I've put in decades of hard work to get to where I am and have had plenty of failures along the way. Through hard work, determination, and the simple fact of never giving up on my dreams, I have reached an incredible place in my life with a beautiful family, and I get all the time I've ever needed to spend with them.

From a very young age, I always had entrepreneurial tendencies. I was a hustler. For example, I was big into collecting sports cards. So, I would have my mother drive me down to the sports card store, and I would borrow $20 from her to buy a box of cards. I would open the entire box of cards right there in front of the store owner with the intention of selling him back all the good cards that came out of the box. Many times, I walked out with double (or more) what my mom gave me, and I gave her the principal loan back right then. Although I didn't actually realize what I was learning or doing at the time, that was my first taste of leverage, debt, profits, and sales.

I was big into sports as a kid. I was always a people pleaser. I always had a lot of friends and was very sociable. But on the inside, I never thought I was good enough. And that right there, my friends, is what actually drove me. Looking back, that feeling of insecurity is what gave me the ambition, desire, and determination to push as hard as I did to reach this place in my life (and I'm not even close to being done).

So, be grateful for who you are, but also know that you can achieve so much more by just doing the work and having the desire. You also need a path to reach your goals, but that's why you're reading this book.

If you're interested in real estate, or you want to create an amazing life for yourself—if you want to buy rentals, have cash flow, and build wealth—then I wrote this book for you. This book is for every stage in your career. It's for the young newbie who wants to be a hustler, **wholesaling** and **fixing and flipping** houses, all the way to someone who is looking to buy rental properties to accumulate wealth and everyone in between. (*Note: bolded terms are explained in detail in the "Terminology" section at the end of the book*)

There is a path for you, whether you want to do this full-time or part-time. This path has been proven possible not only by myself but also by thousands of others across the country. This business can start by simply increasing your income through wholesaling and fixing and flipping, and it can eventually turn into a retirement plan.

In this book, I will tell you the process to take this business from a part-time hustle into a true business that will create abundance beyond your wildest dreams. You will learn the strategy, the plan, the tactics, and the tools that will increase your active income and wealth and build a true retirement plan through real estate—whether you're doing this full-time or part-time. After you read this book, my hope is that you will get involved in real estate investing if you aren't already. This book can help you find the deal, analyze the deal, and exit the deal through wholesaling, fixing and flipping, or buying as a rental. This book is for those who will take action and who know deep down inside that they deserve more.

This book is meant for you.

Pro Tip: Your life is 100% dependent on you. You can choose to live a meager life or an extraordinary one. Stop taking life for granted. We all have our own stories and hardships, but don't use them as excuses for not creating an amazing life. If you can decide what you want and who you need to be to achieve it, you'll realize that much of it often comes at the cost of money. Money does matter. Too often, I and others are criticized for saying that money matters. While I agree that family and moments are important, those moments can be even more incredible when experienced in amazing locations. The point I'm making is that the incredible moments you share with your children and loved ones can be even more amazing if they happen in extraordinary places.

CHAPTER ONE
The Crash and the Comeback

"The greatest things in life all require commitment, sacrifice, some struggle and hardship. It's not easy. But it's absolutely worth it."
– Robin S. Sharma

So, let's rewind the clock, shall we? While attending UCLA in the early 2000s, I met one of my best friends, who is the reason I got into real estate. He and I would work out every day and talk about what we would do once we graduated from college. During our senior year, he asked if I wanted to get into real estate with him and start a **real estate brokerage**. Not only was this an easy decision because he was becoming one of my best friends, but I also knew what his family had been able to build from scratch. Truthfully, I had no real direction as we were finishing up college, but my entrepreneurial mentality made me see this as the ultimate opportunity to not just partner with a good friend of mine but, more importantly, start my adult entrepreneurial journey. I told him, "Hell yes!" So, he told me that once we graduated, I should go waste some time while he got his brokerage license, and then he would call me.

I graduated from UCLA in 2003 and went straight into door-to-door sales. It became my own business and took me across the country to service our client, Verizon. Well, imagine a California boy going door to door in Boston, Massachusetts, in the middle of winter. Let's just say I wasn't built for that.

So, in 2005, I developed pneumonia and had to move all the way back home with my family. Simultaneously, my best friend from UCLA finally called and asked if I wanted to get into real estate. He already knew my answer, but frankly, I knew nothing about real estate yet. All I knew was that billionaires were heavily involved in real estate, and as far as I'm aware, real estate has created the most billionaires. (The interesting part of this data regarding billionaires in real estate is that if you look up those moguls, they often made their big money in a different industry and then went into real estate.) That being said, I liked the thought of taking a path that created billionaires. The fact that I didn't know anything didn't scare me for a second and actually fueled my fire to learn.

So, when I got that call, I immediately jumped to it. While I felt like I was, quite literally, on my proverbial deathbed, I started studying for the real estate exam. It took me roughly ninety days to get enough energy and study power to be ready to take the exam. I was never a good test taker in school, so honestly, I was nervous. But I passed the test. I don't remember the score I got, but I passed on my first attempt. As a side note, these tests are ridiculous. The information you are tested on has little to no real-world use. A **REALTOR**® is in the people business, just like any good salesperson is. As a philosophy, I just want the

Ferrari; I don't need to know exactly how the engine works as long as it's fast!

Here I was, licensed and ready to get involved in real estate. My friend and I started a boutique brokerage in Northern California. During those years (between 2005 and 2006), real estate was on fire. It was an incredible time to be in the industry. Although I was young, I did know that, in a "regular" economy, the real estate market was not this amazing. It felt like the Wild West. The banks were giving out 100 percent loans, and there was free money flowing everywhere. It didn't matter how much money you made or what your credit score was—it seemed like they gave out money to anyone with a heartbeat. So, I was blessed to be in a scenario where my friend's father was a home developer, and we were able to sell his new home builds.

Because of the booming economy, it was anything but an actual sales job. Every day, I would go into a new home build, sit behind the desk in one of the models, literally have five to twenty offers, and simply take the highest offer each and every day. There was no negotiating involved. It wasn't my job to find buyers and lenders or market the development. My job was simply to show the product to the buyer and ask if they were going to make an offer. Well, that led to great income and the ability for me to buy my first home for $500,000, a $100,000 car, and expensive furniture. I literally went to work every day with zero skill set.

Let me expand a bit on not having a skill set. I actually had an amazing skill set, which was my ability to deal with people. I was incredible with people. I asked questions, I listened, I empathized, and

I offered assistance. However, I didn't actually have a process, a system, a strategy, or a technique for what I was doing. I was just going off pure innate ability, and we all know that can only take you so far. It was a mistake to rely solely on natural talent, and it continues to be a mistake for those who are trying to be the best, make more money, or simply do better.

Let me give you a couple of prominent examples: Stephen Curry, LeBron James, and Michael Jordan. They all have natural abilities. They are all athletic. But without technique, relentless practice on their craft, or a coach to tell them where to make adjustments, none of these incredible athletes would be who they are today. Your skill set becomes your craft, and you must *perfect* your craft.

You need to always look for ways to improve your skill set, whether through books like this or coaching, mentoring, masterminds, or podcasts. If you're not *continuously* improving, you will be left behind. You might be able to make some money, but you will never reach your potential without learning and adapting.

The Five Pillars of Success

As I started looking for ways to improve my skills and began to climb the ladder of success, I followed a five-step program. I'm eager to share with you the "five pillars of success" that prepared me and propelled me forward. These steps will set you up to be successful.

1. **Decide what you want and who you need to be in order to achieve it.** This will take you some time. In other words, don't

make a quick decision while reading this book. You need to understand what you want your life to look like in order to make this decision. You need to figure out what you're trying to create and how you would like to create it. You need to realize the sacrifices you'll have to make. Take a moment and write out what your perfect day looks like. I don't mean, you know, I wake up at nine, I play with my kid. I'm saying write out your perfect day in detail. This will not be easy. You will need to dig deep. It should be as granular as the smell of the air, the temperature outside, etc. This should become very emotional for you. Because if you know what that looks like, then you'll start to understand what you need to create to achieve it. *You must be willing to do whatever it takes to get what you want.* So, if you make a decision to be a successful real estate investor who earns a million dollars a year and has a hundred-million-dollar net worth, you have to understand what you have to do to get there. How much time do you need to invest in it, how much sacrifice do you need to make, and how much money do you need to invest in it? You need to become the version of yourself who has a hundred-million-dollar net worth and makes millions every year.

2. **Commit to it.** This is where the rubber meets the road, ladies and gentlemen. You need to commit to it. I know a lot of people give me lip service. They say they're committed; they'll do whatever it takes, and when push comes to shove, they make excuses. So, it's as simple as this: Can you look at yourself in the mirror, make the sacrifices, work seven days a week, even

on holidays, for what you want? Can you sacrifice TV, video games, hanging out with friends, and going to clubs? And for those of you who are doing this part-time, the sacrifice is to invest more of your time. When you get home from work, you have to do more work to achieve a greater result. This is where you need to stay committed.

3. **Take massive action.** I would rather people repeatedly take blind or imperfect actions and try to improve them than spend their time planning or waiting for the perfect time to begin to act. *You need to take action more than you need to plan.* For many of you, this will be a challenge. It is better for you to take the wrong action and learn from it than to wait too long to take the right action and miss the opportunity to learn along the way. Simply put, take massive imperfect action, get results, and perfect along the way.

4. **Be extremely uncomfortable.** Let me put it this way: When you were a child, it was uncomfortable to learn how to walk. Then, it was uncomfortable to learn how to ride a bike. And if you learned how to swim, that was uncomfortable, too. Everything we achieve in life is initially uncomfortable. But with repetition, you become used to it, and it gets more comfortable with time. When starting out on this journey, reasonably speaking, you're going to be uncomfortable. No one likes to be uncomfortable, and in my opinion, this has to do with the fear of failure, and that fear of failure really stems from the fear of judgment. Those who truly succeed in business

allow themselves to fail along the way because it is the only way to grow. Learning how to walk, how to ride a bike, and how to swim is no different from learning how to find your first investment property, how to talk directly with sellers, and how to negotiate a deal. It may be out of your comfort zone, but if you take the mentality we had as children, then you will keep going until you achieve it.

5. **Remove the time expectation of achieving results.** This is the biggest challenge I see when mentoring and coaching the Science of Flipping community, as they all want results before they even play the game. Many want to get a deal in thirty days. While that's technically achievable, they aren't willing to put in the work it will take to get that deal done. They would rather make excuses. So, when people expect the results to come in faster than the time it takes to put the work into it, they end up quitting because they don't think it's achievable. If you say, "I'm going to get my first deal in the first thirty days," and you don't, then you're going to be discouraged and will likely give up. But if you say, "I'm going to get my first deal as fast as I can," you're less likely to quit, even if it takes you thirty, sixty, ninety days or longer. Removing the time expectation to achieve results is about patience. We, as a culture, lack patience these days. We live in a microwave society where people want immediate gratification. We get all fired up about something and expect to see results overnight. I call it having "aggressive patience." *Be aggressive when setting goals and taking action to achieve them, but be patient when reaching the results.*

The Financial Collapse

The start of 2007 was also the start of my downfall. We all know what happened. The market turned and inevitably crashed. I lost it all, including that new home I'd just bought. And the repo man took my car.

On a side note, the story of the car repossession is sort of funny. I didn't realize it was a federal offense to take your car across state lines and trade it with someone else to make sure the repo man couldn't actually find your car. So, I did just that. My best friend and I traded cars with each other. He was in Arizona, I was in California, and they could not find our cars. Well, enough became enough when they went after my family, and so, finally, I handed over the car to the repo man. So, here I was, sleeping on my friend's couch, having lost it all, thinking, *What the hell do I do?*

The one thing I did know was that I loved real estate. The issue was that I didn't enjoy being a REALTOR®. As a REALTOR®, you are a service provider, your clients are your bosses, and that did not sit well with me. I always felt like a servant when I was working with buyers. I would send them properties I thought they would be interested in, and they would schedule a time for us to go look at them. I would spend hours at a time with people who ultimately were just looking and were not serious about buying, which became a waste of time.

On the flip side, there were sellers who became desperate because of the economy, and they were **over-leveraged**. They couldn't sell their home to a buyer for a price the buyers were willing to pay. Once again, it was a lot of time wasted with no reward at the end. To be fair, if I had the skill set dialed in, I don't believe this would have been the case. So, I decided that **real estate investing** would be a much more enjoyable route. There was only one, or maybe two, shows on TV about flipping houses, so it wasn't nearly as popular as it is today, but it had 100 percent of my attention. This wasn't an "aha" moment, but I thought, *I'm going to be a successful real estate investor!*

So, while there are many very successful REALTORS® in the world, most of those same REALTORS® have an investing arm to their business. They understand what I realized at that moment: that you can make a lot more money flipping homes and being your own boss than you could by listing a property and making 3 percent. Flippers typically aim to make 10 percent or more. That is a massive difference in income.

In 2007, YouTube, Facebook, and other social media sites were not nearly as big as they are today. This was well before services such as Zillow, Redfin, PropStream, REI Lead Machine, and Privy. So, while I had no coach at the time, no mentor, and no one for me to rely on or ask questions to, I went to Starbucks daily and started calling REALTORS® from www.Realtor.com.

Let me give you a little fun fact about Starbucks. Not only did I just go there to get hopped up on all the caffeine I could drink, but in 2007, as long as you stayed inside the shop, they would give you free refills. Obviously, I didn't have a whole lot of money to buy $5 or $7 lattes. So, I got the cheapest black coffee I could, called REALTORS®, and asked for refills as often as I wanted. I couldn't even afford their snacks, so my friend would fill up a bag of almonds because they're healthy and high in protein, and essentially, I would sit there, slamming coffee and eating my almonds all day while I called REALTORS®.

You might be asking, "Why is this story relevant?" Well, it's because not having enough money to break into real estate investing isn't a valid excuse. It's actually not about the *resources* you have; it's about being *resourceful* yourself. You'll hear more about this throughout the book.

Calling REALTORS® to make offers on homes listed on the **multiple listing services (MLS)** database—the same strategy that I used when I was broke, busted, and disgusted—is the same strategy I use now after making millions of dollars. It's actually one of our best strategies, and it's a method that I teach my entire Science of Flipping Community to get their first deals. The Science of Flipping Community is my coaching community, where I show our members how to build financial freedom through active participation in real estate. But sixteen years ago, it was the *only* strategy that I could think of to try and find my first investment deal. And because I had no money, this was a free way to be resourceful without having the means to go find my first deal.

Becoming a Hustler

Back in 2007, I figured out what I wanted, and I decided who I needed to be to get it. It was clear I wanted to be a really successful real estate investor who makes millions of dollars with a massive rental portfolio. I was a full-time hustler, so I just went through the Rolodex of REALTORS® in Phoenix, Arizona, and started cold calling agents to tell them that I was interested in making an offer on their listing without even knowing whether or not they had one.

Whether you want to be a part-time hustler or you're planning on a full-time business, I will share with you exactly how to find the deals, how to analyze the deals, and how to exit the deals. You just need a process and a plan to take action on every day. You will likely want a coach, a mentor, or an adviser to help you. I will give you all of my resources and processes, as well as the tools, skills, and strategy to implement them.

NOTE: *Be on the lookout for QR codes at the end of each chapter to scan and download to get additional resources to execute immediately.*

Before we wrap up this chapter, let me tell you the story about the difference between *having* resources versus *being* resourceful. The latter wins every time. So, while I was cold calling these agents, I knew I was missing something, as I wasn't getting much traction. I was months into calling these agents without a deal. So, one day, I found a YouTube video about a real estate seminar. I applied to attend and was accepted. After spending three days in this seminar in San Diego, California, I realized I needed to invest in a coach. It was clear to me that I didn't know what I didn't know. I was flying blind, and although I had plenty of energy, effort, and determination, I had no systems or processes, which made me feel the same way I felt when I was a REALTOR®. I knew I needed to build my skill set, find a process, and find someone to hold my hand. So, when the price tag came up for coaching, you know I didn't have it. But I became resourceful at that moment. I made a call to a friend of mine, who I knew had the money, and begged him to let me borrow $25,000 for coaching. Well, he gave me the $25,000, and it was the best investment I ever made.

Remember, it's not about having the resources; it is always about being resourceful.

> **Pro Tip**: The GREATS possess these 4 attributes:
>
> 1. *Belief* - They believe it before they see it.
> 2. *Action* - They take massive action. Not perfect action: they take consistent action.
> 3. *Failure* - They are willing to fail, knowing they will get back up, adapt, innovate, and keep pushing forward.
> 4. *Perseverance* - Regardless of their wins or failures, they keep going and keep pushing forward
>
> Regardless of the talent or skill set you possess, it will always take the work ethic and discipline to get to the highest of mountaintops.

Bonus Resources to Take Action Now!
SCAN THE QR CODE:

CHAPTER TWO

Where to Start

"The best way to predict your future is to create it."
– Abraham Lincoln

I get questions from many of my community members at the Science of Flipping, but the most common question is: Where do I start? So, let's talk about the three ways to go out and find deals.

- Working with agents.
- Marketing directly to the seller.
- Working with other investors.

Working With Agents

The first way, as mentioned in Chapter One, is by working with agents through the MLS. I love this method because it's essentially *free*. You can go into any market in any city, and there will be listings on the MLS for people who want to sell. Now, in the real estate investor space, everyone talks about finding motivated sellers. Well, frankly, there is no higher sign of motivation than when someone lists their property on the MLS and is actively selling their home. Many people try to argue that there are no "deals" on the MLS. Well, I have proven that argument wrong and continue to prove it wrong to this day. Not only did I start out by getting deals through REALTORS® who have properties listed on the MLS, but sixteen years later, I am still making offers on listed properties across the nation. There are services (like Privy) that allow investors like me to have access to over a hundred regional MLS databases across the country. In the past, only licensed agents in that local market were allowed access. These resources give me the ability to call agents on listings in any city where I want to buy homes.

The challenge is that most people don't know how to analyze the property correctly, and they just make lowball offers with some made-up number. There is a lot more to making an offer on the listed properties. First of all, if the property is listed with an agent, then you need to be nice to that agent and not come off like you're just trying to "steal" the home. You want to build rapport with the agent and get information on what is going on with the seller. Building rapport is a skill set that needs to be practiced. It involves questioning, listening, empathizing, understanding, and agreement. There are books written on how to practically build rapport, but the best example I can give you is to care more about the seller than the house. If you ask questions about them and listen and not just try to make an offer, you will start the process of building actual rapport. Not all listed properties are a good investment. Don't forget that agents are basically gatekeepers and are there to protect and service their client (the seller), so finessing the conversation is important. It always comes down to being able to make an offer that *creates value* for the seller and is still *a good buy* for you, the investor.

Marketing Directly to the Seller

The second way to find properties is off-market, where you go directly to the sellers. Now, this chapter isn't necessarily about marketing; however, there are many ways to market directly to sellers. All marketing works—you just have to find the best strategy. Here is an example of marketing to a homeowner: Find the list provider that works for you (I use www.REILeadMachine.com). Next, pull a list of absentee homeowners or a list of owner-occupants. There are fifteen to twenty-five different lists that you can pull. You can target those homeowners through several different strategies, such as cold calling, emailing, direct mailing, door knocking, text messaging, and door hanging. You simply need to pull the list, **skip trace** it (skip tracing is using software to take an address or a person's name and find their contact information) for an email and phone number, and, at a bare minimum, start calling, emailing, and texting those homeowners. Now, when working directly with the homeowner, the one thing we're looking for as real estate investors is "motivation."

Working with Other Investors

The third way to find deals is to bring a buyer (another investor) as a wholesaler to someone else's deal. This means you either find another wholesaler who has already built a relationship with an agent and contracted a deal from the MLS, or you go directly to the homeowner and get the deal under contract. Since the other wholesaler hasn't found a buyer yet, *you* will find a buyer for his deal.

As a side note, it's crucial for all investors to stay informed about the prices other investors are offering and paying for their deals. What criteria are they looking at to make a property a good deal? *The more you know about other buyers, the better pulse you have on the real estate market in general.* This also helps you to act as a personal shopper to active buyers.

So, you have a three-pronged strategy:
1. Work with REALTORS® to buy listed properties.
2. Start marketing to go directly to sellers.
3. Work with other investors.

All three of these strategies can implement automated processes, so you don't always have to do the work. This is why I mentioned that this book was for people who either want to do this full-time or part-time if they have a W-2 job. Those who are reading this book can implement these processes right out of the gate.

Analyzing the Deal

As real estate investors, we look for two specific things: "pain" and "potential." What I mean by "pain" is, typically, financial "pain," such as medical injuries, property tax, and job loss. These are often unfortunate circumstances, and you don't wish them on anyone; however, they are a reality for many. As long as you come to the conversation bringing value to the homeowner, there is often a deal to work out. The seller doesn't want the home to be lost to foreclosure, and while it often takes a long time for a deal to be done, you end up helping out the seller in a major way.

When I talk about "potential," I'm referring to the "potential" of the property. Not just aesthetically but also from a financial perspective. I want to know what the "potential" of the house is in terms of what I can turn it into. Does it need a whole remodel, or does it just need some paint and carpet? Or would it be a better rental or fix-and-flip? We need to analyze everything and look at the financial "potential" of the property to understand the numbers. For that, there are six important questions to think through:

1. Why am I buying the house?
2. How much will it cost me to remodel it?
3. How much can I sell it for after remodeling?
4. How much rent can I charge after remodeling?
5. If I keep the house, how much is my mortgage, interest, taxes, and insurance?
6. How much is the holding cost for the property while I remodel to sell?

If we can offer speed and convenience, more often than not, we don't have to offer top price. We just need to create value for the homeowner so that they want to work with us to sell their home.

Now, many homeowners across the nation don't necessarily have "pain," and many homeowners often don't know the "potential" of their home either. While I love working with absentee homeowners, who are defined as "landlords," working with owner-occupied houses can be advantageous as well. So, let's talk about finding the "potential" in the deal. This all comes down to how you analyze the deal. For example, there are three exit strategies: You can wholesale, you can fix and flip, or you can **buy and hold**. Then, you need to **underwrite** each potential deal in two different ways. Is this a good fix-and-flip, or is this a good buy-and-hold?

Using a Buy Box

A **buy box** is one of the best tools you can use to analyze a possible deal. A buy box accounts for all the costs that go into the home. It is essentially an Excel spreadsheet where you input the appropriate numbers into the fields. This will not only tell you what you are willing to spend, but also how much you will sell it for and what the commissions are. Here is an example of a buy box calculation to see if a property would be a good flip. As you can see, we have three major points: The purchase price, the estimated renovation cost, and the **after-repair value (ARV)**. If that profit box is green like it is here in the image, then it's a "green light" to buy.

Entry Box	
Purchase Price	$140,000
Estimated Renovations	$50,000
ARV	$279,000
Market Rent	$1,800

QUICK FLIP CALCULATOR

Purchase Price	$140,000		
Total Hold Time in # Months	6	After Repair Value	$279,000.00
Purchase Related Costs	$0	Repair Costs	**$50,000.00**
Finance Cost Per Month	$1,900	Cost Over Runs	$2,500.00
Taxes Per Month	$93	Finance Cost	$11,400.00
Insurance Per Month	$117	Carrying Costs	$3,360.00
Other Expense Per Month Uitlities	$350	**Total Holding Costs**	**$14,760.00**
Repair Costs Margin of Error	5%	Selling Costs	$13,950.00
Renovation Estimate	$50,000	Closing Tilte + Attorney/Other	$3,500.00
Commissions Cost For Selling	5%	**Total Selling Costs**	**$17,450.00**
Closing Title + Attorney & Other M	$3,500	**Total Expenses**	**$84,710.00**
ARV	$279,000	**Profit**	**54,290.00**

26

Short-Term, Long-Term and Mid-Term Rentals

These days, the **buy-and-hold** category has **short-term rentals**, **long-term rentals**, and **mid-term rentals** as three separate ways to analyze those deals. I always start by working with long-term rentals. Does this property work for a long-term rental? Certain price points make this very difficult. Price points above $300,000 tend to make a long-term rental very challenging. However, price points between $300,000 all the way up to $5 million can create a great short-term rental market. Price points between $300,000 and $700,000 can create a great mid-term rental market. Again, it is how you analyze the deal.

Here is an image of a good buy box calculation for a long-term rental:

LONG TERM RENTAL CALCULATOR

Purchase data			Purchase data			Monthly Net Operating Income		
Purchase Price ($)		$140,000	New ARV Purchase Price ($)		$279,000	Gross Rental Income	$2,600	
Repairs/Renovation ($)		$50,000						
Closing Costs ($)		$6,800	**Loan data**			Property Management		$234
Down Payment		$28,000	Max Refi Amount		$209,250	Maintenance		$50
Project Capital Needed		$59,800	New Amount Financed ($)		$203,280	Property Taxes		$116
Rehab Loan Amt		$162,000	Refi Loan Monthly Payment		(1,463.11)	Insurance		$233
Monthly Debt Coverage		$1,620				Total Expenses		$633
			Total Acquisition, Rehab and Holding Costs					
			Total Invested		$196,800	Net Operating Income	$1,967	
			Holding Costs		$6,480			
			Total		$203,280	**Cashflow**	Monthly	Annual
						Net Operating Income	$1,967	$23,807
						Principal and Interest	$(1,463)	$(17,557)
			Potential Cash Out at Refi		$5,970	Cashflow	$ 504	$ 6,050
			Equity Position		$75,720			

All the same data points, such as purchase price, estimated rehab cost, and ARV, are calculated. The other point will be rental income after remodeling. If the three boxes at the bottom turn green, as shown here, then it's a "green light" for a good rental. My personal buy box must have a minimum of $200 per month net rental income, 20 percent equity, and a 20 percent cash-on-cash return. If my calculations are right and I purchase the home, I'll be able to take all my money out of the property when I refinance, as I prefer and believe the "**BRRRR**" model (**Buy, Rehab, Rent, Refinance, Repeat**) to be the best investing model out there.

I just gave you a better understanding of a long-term rental, and I can briefly discuss the short-term and midterm rental models. The short-term (STR) model has had a great run as a profitable business model, as you can charge premiums for rent for short-term stays. However, as I write this book, the STR model has cooled off a bit; it became oversaturated, and government policies started challenging the model and locations. (To make sure you have the correct and most up-to-date information, I would always check with www.Airbnb.com and www.YourCity.gov.) The STR model still has legs, but you'd better be familiar with the market and neighborhood where you buy that property.

The market for mid-term rentals is starting to gain more traction. Historically this market has been known as "executive rentals," as there was a focus on executives or traveling nurses who had to do short-term stints of over thirty days in that location. There has been a push into this model because it also has long-term, higher-than-average rental rates and can turn a property that might not be a great long-term rental into a cash cow as a mid-term rental.

Now, I don't want to confuse you in this chapter, but there are separate ways to analyze each and all of these models. Resources on this topic can also be found if you scan the QR code found at the end of this chapter. So, as you look at each and every home, you need to understand the best exit. Do you have a buyer lined up, or are you going to flip it? Will someone else keep it, or will you? Will it be kept as a long-term rental, short-term rental, or mid-term rental?

A quick note here: As I'm writing this book, I have been able to implement AI into my direct-to-seller marketing. It's absolutely amazing. The marketing strategy is based on my online presence and my website. Sellers who go to my website are automatically pulled into my CRM (customer relationship manager), or they can opt-in. Either way, automation and AI start the conversation and take it all the way to making the offer. This technology is cutting-edge. You can find it at www.Rocketly.ai. At the time I'm writing this book, you can schedule a demo and check it out yourself.

Using Automation

Here is an example of a process our business uses right now. Our CRM has built-in automation, and we utilize AI. The combination of automation and AI begins to communicate with each and every seller we bring into our customer relationship management software (CRM), so we don't need to hire people to do this. This can be very helpful for those who want to do this part-time. You do not need to be on the phone all day long to start talking to a salesperson. Just implement some of the automation and AI that are already available. The process to find that deal starts with having an online presence. Our website (developed by www.MinutePages.com) brings sellers into our CRM because we have an opt-in for those who want to sell their house fast and those who want to sell their house with no commissions. This way, they can chat directly with us.

Not to go even deeper into the trenches, but our website has technology that helps us capture contact information on our visitors. They don't even need to opt in for us to get their information. We will get 10 to 50 percent of those people who are simply looking at our website, and they will transfer over to our CRM. So, in the example that one hundred people view our website, we will get thirty people's names, email addresses, and phone numbers, and it will allow our automation and AI to start a conversation with those people.

Analyzing the Property

Finding the property is one thing, but analyzing the property is an entirely different skill. How you analyze the property comes down to your exit strategy. Is this property a better fix-and-flip, rental, or wholesale deal? Here are some questions you will want to ask:

- Is there profit in the middle after you or someone else buys it, rehabs it, and sells it on the market after commissions and **closing costs**?

- If there isn't, is it still at a price point that makes a good rental?

Now, I'm going to pause here, as I think most people reading are wondering, "Where do I get the money from if it's a good flip or a good rental?"

As I've mentioned before, you don't need your own money to buy a flip, nor do you need your own money to buy a rental. There are companies out there called **hard money** lenders, which will lend you 75 or 80 percent of your purchase price, and you will need to bring 25, 20, 15, or 10 percent cash down to fund the deal. Those same hard money lenders will reimburse you for your rehab budget if you're remodeling, but you will still need cash to get started. So, a good mathematical equation would be: You will need roughly 30 to 40 percent of the purchase price in cash if you're going to rehab it.

Now, I highly suggest finding people who would like to be in the real estate game with you. I like using retirement account money as a way for other people to earn money as a lender for me on my fix-and-flips and rentals in the very short term until I refinance with a bank loan. You can do the same. You just need the process to find those people, know what to say, and understand how to structure it.

Let me give you an example of when I made a decision to buy a home because it was a great flip but also a great rental, and I didn't use any of my own money to buy it. I have a property in Jacksonville, Florida that I bought with the full intention of buying and holding. It needed a full-blown rehab. We had another investor—which is one of the ways to find deals—send us this house. We bought it from him, he made an assignment fee, and everyone felt good. We remodeled the deal, but the city stopped us because there were some plumbing issues. So, we couldn't continue the model until my contractors fixed these issues. Because of the ninety-day delay, the interest rates went up, and it no longer made sense to keep it as a rental. But because we calculated with a buy box and bought the home right, there was plenty of profit in there for us to fix and flip the property. So, we did just that. We finished our remodel, put it up for sale, and sold it on the MLS for a profit. This is a perfect example of a property you will want to find that fits both models—properties that can either be a good rental or a good fix-and-flip.

Now that I've shown you an example of how I bought a property from another investor, the key takeaway from this chapter is to understand that I didn't spend any of my own money. We didn't have a team going out there to hunt for deals. For those of you who are just getting started, you want to be in markets that are well under 30 percent of the national average, which is, at the time I'm writing this book, currently around $400,000. I suggest you target markets that are at least 30 percent under that amount.

You, too, can have a successful deal without using your own money.

Pro Tip: Remember, real estate is a people business and always will be. You are dealing with the biggest financial investment and decision in people's lives. You can use as much AI as you want, but it will never replace getting on the phone with someone to help them find a solution. Refining your analysis and using AI can help immensely, but this business is going to come down to how many people you talk to (Homeowners and Agents) and how many offers you make. If you remember that, then you will win the game of real estate.

Download My Personal Buy Box and Scripts for Sellers and Agents.

SCAN THE QR CODE:

CHAPTER THREE

Finding Your Next Deal

"Your time is limited, don't waste it living someone else's life."
– Steve Jobs

In Chapter Two, we discussed the three ways to find a deal: working with agents, marketing directly to owners, and working with other investors. So, let's start off with the least risky way—buying from other investors.

Working With Investors

There are many other investors across the nation who spend a lot of money in marketing to find these deals. These investors tend to be wholesalers, and there are several social media platforms where you can find them. When they submit a deal to you, similar to how a real estate agent has a listing, they have a potential deal to sell the contract, which would be called an **assignment contract**. You would make an offer on these deals at a number that works for you. This number should be enough to buy the home as a fix-and-flip or as a rental. Again, it's all about how you analyze the property.

There will be times when investors will deny your offers because, honestly, those wholesalers haven't done a good enough job getting the property under contract at a low enough price that makes sense for a fix-and-flipper or a landlord buyer. Many experienced investors miss this strategy and believe they need to be the ones to find their own deals. Well, I will tell you now that they're missing out. And if you, yourself, are an experienced investor, listen up. You need to start making offers on other wholesalers' deals. Offers that will suit you. Offers that will fit landlord-type investors. There are tens of thousands of investors out there who can find their own deals; you just need to make the offer. That is just the first way to find deals.

Working With REALTORS®

The next would be with REALTORS®. There are two strategies when working with REALTORS®. First, you can simply make an offer on their personal listing. The second strategy is for them to become essentially **bird dogs** for off-market properties that they would consider **pocket listings**.

REALTORS® have a similar job as investors. Just like investors go out to find deals, REALTORS® go out to find listings. However, REALTORS® often come across properties that are not ideal listings. These properties are usually outdated, haven't been updated for over thirty years, or require a lot of work.

Many times, REALTORS® don't know what to do with a property they have a listing appointment for. This is when investors can develop a relationship with the REALTOR® and say, "Hey, we're looking for damaged property," or "We're looking for property that needs to be value-added. That is our target property. So, [Mr. or Mrs. REALTOR®], when you come across these properties in your listing appointments, please call us. We'll make sure you get paid a commission on this property."

One of my REALTOR® outreach specialists was doing his job finding agents with listings. He called an agent with a listing that he knew would not be a good fit for his investment strategy, but he wanted to start the relationship. He asked some pretty basic questions, such as:

- Why are the sellers looking to sell?

- How long have they lived there?

- Is the neighborhood more of an owner-occupied neighborhood or a landlord-rental neighborhood?

- Has the seller remodeled any part of the house, and how long ago?

The agent said that a couple of weeks prior, she'd met with someone who had a house that wasn't in good condition and wouldn't make a good listing. My specialist said properties like that are exactly what we were looking for. He made the point to the REALTOR® that she could represent us on the purchase and that she could earn a commission. The REALTOR® then brought our offer to the seller with a short inspection contingency, and the seller signed. The agent was so happy, as she got paid two sides of a commission on something she thought was dead. From that point forward, she kept sending us deals to review for our model.

The point is that we started the relationship without knowing whether we'd get a deal, and we ended up closing a deal in just two weeks.

In this sense, REALTORS® are working as a bird dog for you. You become a "value add" to the REALTOR®—a tool in the REALTOR®'s belt. So, they love the fact that you can help them make money from an appointment they might not have made much from without you. So, it is always good to reach out to real estate agents and let them know you're looking for value-added properties that need to be fixed up.

Now, the direct strategy with REALTORS® is to call them and have a conversation about their active listing. Why is it still active? Why hasn't it sold? The key with REALTORS®, investors, and sellers is to build a relationship. One thing to understand is that this is their livelihood, too, and they need to make money. So, if you can show them that value (that by working with us, they will make money), you will build a close relationship. Not every listing is a good investment property, and not every REALTOR® enjoys working with investors. You will have to do some digging to find a REALTOR® who enjoys and knows how to work with investors. And just because you've built a relationship with a REALTOR®, it doesn't mean they'll accept your offer because the seller makes the final decision to accept it or not.

Many of you might be asking yourself, *What do I say to these REALTORS®?* There are multiple ways to speak to the REALTOR®

depending on the listing or whether they will be your bird dog. There are ways to show why you're making an offer that is under list price. You'll need to show value not just to the REALTOR® but to the seller, and sometimes that value can be speed and sometimes convenience. While each of these conversations has a bit of nuance, for the most part, the point of every conversation that you have with a REALTOR® should be about the relationship you can build moving forward and not just about the single listing you are calling about. Remember, the agents are thinking, *What's in it for me?* in these conversations, so make sure you tell them.

Here is an example of a property that was listed on the MLS with a REALTOR® (my company bought this property at exactly the listed price). We hired a new twenty-one-year-old kid to come work for us in acquisitions. His first role after training was to reach out to REALTORS® and make offers on listed properties. One of the things he asked us was if he could have our buy box. (This was our buy box from the spreadsheet I showed you earlier.)

Entry Box	
Purchase Price	$140,000
Estimated Renovations	$50,000
ARV	$279,000
Market Rent	$1,800

He called a REALTOR®, had a discussion using our negotiating tactics, and put those four numbers into our buy box. And if the profit box turned green, then he would make an offer, even if it was at list price. And if the rental profit and the equity portion turned green on the rental model, he would make an offer to the agent even if it was at list price. (For reference, see the entire buy box in Chapter 4.)

So, we bought a property at $99,900, which is the exact list price the REALTOR® had set. Because of that price (based on the rehab value, the ARV, and the rental income), the property was a deal. It didn't matter that we were buying it at the list price.

A key takeaway from this story was that this twenty-one-year-old guy didn't know anything about real estate, but he followed the process. And because of that, he made a substantial commission.

Off-Market Properties

So, let's dive into the third way to get a deal and what most investors think is the holy grail of deals—off-market properties. This is where you go directly to the seller.

Some of my favorite ways to go directly to the seller are:

- Pay-per-click marketing on Google
- Pay-per-click marketing on Facebook
- Cold calls
- Email
- Direct mail

One time, a seller from Europe who owned a property in Detroit found our website through our Facebook ads. She filled out her information so we could contact her. As usual, our automation and AI reached out via email, and they began communicating. It got to a point where she asked for an offer, and the alerts went off for our acquisition team to figure out what the offer would be. So, we emailed her our best offer. She asked for a little more money. We denied that, and she eventually agreed on our number. After inspecting the home, we realized the project was a lot bigger than we thought, and there was a tenant who wasn't paying rent. So, for the headaches we were about to have, we asked for a reduction in price, and she accepted it over email. Keep in mind that no one from my team had actually talked to her; she lived in Europe. So, I immediately reached out to one of my community members from Detroit. He wholesaled many properties per month, so I knew I could count on him to help me sell this property. He agreed to work with us. He found a buyer, and we split almost $30,000 in a wholesale assignment fee on a property where the seller lived in Europe and whom we'd had no personal contact with except for email.

There are two reasons why I find this to be such a great story. First is the community factor. I'm a firm believer that, in order to go from good to great, you need to focus on people. For over sixteen years, I have intentionally focused on building a strong and wide community in the real estate space. That includes REALTORS®, other investors, lenders, title companies, and contractors. The amount of money I've made and the volume of deals I've done just from having that community is immeasurable. Also, no one likes to be a lone wolf. Being part of a community provides comfort and confidence. I know that no matter what I'm faced with, someone in my network and community can help me resolve it.

The second is because I was using automation and technology, I didn't need to have someone doing it personally. The www.MinutePages.com website is created specifically for real estate investors and answers many of the sellers' questions. So, by the time they get to us, they'll be informed that we will pay cash and that we have the ability to close quickly. Then, our automation starts a conversation that sounds just like a human, although there's no manpower behind it. In this case, it led to almost $30,000 in profit that we shared with the other wholesaler, who is actually part of the Science of Flipping community. If you don't have an online presence, you need to. It all starts with your website. In my opinion, www.MinutePages.com offers the best websites for real estate investors. Once you have the website up, you should at least have a process to point traffic to that website. Using Facebook or Google to run inexpensive ads will do the trick. From there, you definitely should have some level of AI communication in your process. I encourage you to take a look at www.Rocketly.ai, and you can book a demo. These days, AI is a very real asset in your process and system. It is too expansive for me to talk about in this book, but you *must* start learning about it.

When most people hear about a new person, company, or idea, they use Google to learn more. If you don't have an online presence, you will miss that homeowner who just googled "how to sell their house fast or for cash." You will miss the people who are looking for us as investors because we offer a service that can make the transaction speedy and convenient.

However, having a website does not necessarily mean people are just going to find you. There are two ways you can do paid marketing: Facebook or Google pay-per-click (PPC). You can also set up a direct email with your website. You can use other social media groups and platforms. Marketing directly to the seller is always a good idea, as there are always people in financial "pain." If you can find these people, you can give them a valuable opportunity that will also give you a great deal. On top of that, having an online presence will help you find people who don't know the "potential" of their own home because they don't want to do the work. All three of these strategies—REALTORS®, investors, and marketing to sellers directly—will work. You will need to choose at least two of these strategies, if not all three. Now, before you complain about your time limitations, I promise that with the right strategy and process, you won't need to do this full-time. I work with REALTORS® and investors, and I do direct-to-seller marketing. This is how you build the opportunity to make a lot of money in active income through wholesaling and rehab flipping and build wealth for your portfolio.

Pro Tip: Growing an investment business comes down to one essential data point…

How many offers did you make today?

There are three basic ways to find a deal

1. Direct to Seller.
2. Through Agents.
3. Doing a JV deal with another investor.

As you go on your journey to find your first or next deal, just know that you need to make offers on all the properties you're interested in; otherwise, there will be no deal.

Scan to Access Video Trainings on How to Properly Analyze a Deal.
SCAN THE QR CODE:

CHAPTER FOUR

Deal or No Deal?

"Opportunities come infrequently. When it rains gold, put out the bucket, not the thimble."
– Warren Buffett

One of my Science of Flipping community members, Anthony, found a property in his own market in Birmingham, Alabama. He is a flipper, and I've been coaching him on how to grow his company. He came across a property that would have been a great flip for him. However, given that his crews were already booked and he was tight on capital, he called me to ask if I would be interested in buying that home. He underwrote the property in a way that he knew the numbers made sense for me to buy it as a good investment. He said, "Justin, go check out the spreadsheet. These are the numbers, and it works for your buy box. Are you interested?" Without hesitation, I said, "Yes." Little did I know that he was making $33,000 on the assignment until I closed the transaction and signed the closing documents.

Seller		Description	Borrower/Buyer	
Debit	Credit		Debit	Credit
		Financial		
	$108,000.00	Sales Price of Property	$108,000.00	
		Constuction Holdback	$65,000.00	
		Deposit including earnest money		$1,000.00
		Loan Amount		$142,800.00
$33,000.00		Assignment Fee to Hudson Homes		

I immediately gave him a call and congratulated him. I couldn't have been happier for him, as I love seeing my community members win. Not only that, but I was able to buy another rental.

This story highlights two important rules:

1. **Understand your buy box.** Understand what makes a deal for you, whether you'll hold it or fix and flip it.

2. **Understand your buyer's buy box.** Where are the buyers buying? At what price? At what percentage of ARV? What type of rental return are they shooting for? You need to know the answers to these questions.

Anthony knew my buy box, and he understood exactly where I could "green light" this property. So, he basically called me, knowing he would offer it to me and that I would say yes. And as a wholesaler, that is exactly the type of relationship you want to have. You want to know your buyer's buy box so intimately that you know all you need to do is call a buyer or two, and the home will be sold. That is a great wholesaler.

Here are some more examples of buy boxes. The first image is for a rehab flip, and the second image is for a long-term rental.

Rehab Flip:

Entry Box	
Purchase Price	$156,000
Estimated Renovations	$40,000
ARV	$300,000
Market Rent	$2,500

QUICK FLIP CALCULATOR

Purchase Price	$156,000		
Total Hold Time In # Months	6	After Repair Value	$300,000.00
Purchase Related Costs	$0	Repair Costs	$40,000.00
Finance Cost Per Month	$1,960	Cost Over Runs	$2,000.00
Taxes Per Month	$104	Finance Cost	$11,760.00
Insurance Per Month	$130	Carrying Costs	$3,504.00
Other Expense Per Month Utilities	$350	**Total Holding Costs**	**$15,264.00**
Repair Costs Margin of Error	5%	Selling Costs	$15,000.00
Renovation Estimate	$40,000	Closing Title + Attorney/Other	$3,900.00
Commissions Cost For Selling	5%	**Total Selling Costs**	**$18,900.00**
Closing Title + Attorney & Other M	$3,900	**Total Expenses**	**$76,164.00**
ARV	$300,000	**Profit**	**67,836.00**

Long Term Rental:

LONG TERM RENTAL CALCULATOR

Purchase data		Purchase data		Monthly Net Operating Income		
Purchase Price ($)	$156,000	New ARV Purchase Price ($)	$300,000	Gross Rental Income	$2,500	
Repairs/Renovation ($)	$40,000			Property Management		$225
Closing Costs ($)	$7,120	Loan data		Maintenance		$50
Down Payment	$31,200	Max Refi Amount	$225,000	Property Taxes		$125
Project Capital Needed	$58,320	New Amount Financed ($)	$209,712	Insurance		$250
Rehab Loan Amt	$164,800	Refi Loan Monthly Payment	(1,573.23)	Total Expenses		$650
Monthly Debt Coverage	$1,648					
		Total Acquisition, Rehab and Holding Costs		Net Operating Income	$1,850	
		Total Invested	$203,120			
		Holding Costs	$6,592	Cashflow	Monthly	Annual
		Total	$209,712	Net Operating Income	$1,850	$22,200
				Principal and Interest	$ (1,573)	$ (18,879)
		Potential Cash Out at Refi	$15,289	Cashflow	$ 277	$ 3,321
		Equity Position	$90,288			

Those are some numbers, but that doesn't give a detailed picture of how the property really is going to perform. This is what you need to account for:

- How long will you hold the property?

- What is the interest rate on your hard money if you have it?

- What is the interest rate on your private money if you have it?

- Calculate how much cost you'll put into the property, given how long you will hold it.

- How much will you put into the remodel?

- Will you do a paint-and-lipstick job, or will you do a full-blown remodel?

My personal strategy is to do a full-blown remodel on every property I buy, but that isn't everyone's plan. So, you need to understand how much money you will be putting into the property. If you plan to sell it as a rehab, you need to understand the cost of selling it, such as REALTOR® commissions, closing costs, and **title** and **escrow** fees.

Once you understand your buy box, you can make better decisions, which helps you negotiate better on the front end. For example, if you know where your bottom-line number is, you wouldn't want to fix and flip a property unless you can make a $50,000 net gross after closing costs, commissions, and all fees are paid. In other words, you'll want to net $50,000 to do a fix-and-flip. If you put the numbers into your buy box and it comes to $32,000, you know you'll not buy it for a fix-and-flip and that you'll essentially need to get an $18,000 reduction on your offer price so that you can net $50,000. Knowing your end number helps you acquire more properties. Anthony and all my community members know that if they just put the numbers in this buy box spreadsheet, they will know how much they can offer. It is important to know what specific buyers want. Their pricing allows you to be a killer acquisition person and will help you contract more deals. You don't need a formula. You can just plug in the numbers and let them speak to you.

For example, I don't want to buy a rental property if I don't net at least $200 per month. I also want to have at least 25 percent equity once I buy the home, remodel the home, and refinance. When I refinance, I want to pull out all the money I put into the home during remodel. There are three items in my buy box:

- Monthly rental income
- Equity position
- Cash-out refinance

Now, what is the importance of my The Science Of Flipping community members having my buy box? I'm not the only buyer out there. Well, it is because if I'm willing to buy it, they know that someone else is willing to buy it or that they themselves should be willing to buy it. It also gives them a little flexibility to know if Justin is a "bougie" flipper (which I am), that someone else might do that flip for $35,000 that Justin Colby won't do unless he makes $50,000, but they're close. So, they may still want to contract the property as a wholesaler and find a buyer who would do it for a net $35,000 as a fix-and-flip. You can just plug in the four numbers—the purchase price, the rehab price, the ARV, and rents—and it spits out where your offer needs to be based on the criteria.

It is important to know not only your own buy box but also the other person's buy box.

Pro Tip: Properly analyzing a deal can make the difference between getting a deal done and passing on a deal. To have a successful real estate business, you need to monetize all the leads you are given. So, in the example that there is a property you may pass on yourself, but that property came to you through your paid marketing, then you need to find another buyer for that deal so that you can at least monetize that deal. This is how the pros can have such a large marketing budget.

Scan for All the Deal Analysis Calculators.
SCAN THE QR CODE:

CHAPTER FIVE

Money Now or Money Later—or Both

"If you do what you've always done, you'll get what you've always gotten."
– Tony Robbins

By now, many of you are trying to figure out: *What should my strategy be? What is the best exit strategy? How do I get started?* So, let's dive into developing your strategy.

As I've mentioned in previous chapters, there are essentially three methods:

1. You can wholesale a property to a different buyer.
2. Fix and flip it.
3. Buy and hold it.

The three buy-and-hold strategies are:

1. Short-term.
2. Long-term.
3. Mid-term (think traveling nurses, people that need more than thirty days to live in a property).

Those three verticals all have separate buckets. So, let's start with the end in mind.

Wholesaling

Remember Pillar 1? *Decide what you want and who you need to be to get it.* Now, if you're a newbie reading this, I highly encourage you to increase your active income. This means that I recommend that you wholesale first because you have little to no risk. Wholesaling is a simple process to market a deal. You're going out there to find opportunities, whether it be with a REALTOR®, another investor, or directly to a homeowner. You need to line up that opportunity with a buyer who wants to buy it. More often than not, you will make an assignment fee, but you also can do something called the **double close**, where your end buyer will fund your purchase and their purchase simultaneously with two separate escrows. This is totally legal and helps to avoid any confusion with the seller on why you're assigning the deal.

Another option to close on a wholesale deal is something called "transactional funding." This is a lender giving you 100 percent lending on your purchase for 24–48 hours max, which then allows your buyer to come and fund his deal with you as the seller within two days. Wholesaling gives you the ability to control the property and then assign your interest in that property to your end buyer.

Here are the advantages of wholesaling:

- You can do it anywhere, even from your couch.
- You have little to no risk.

- It can increase active income.
- It can be done part-time.
- You don't need a big team or operation.
- And most of all, you take on almost no risk and need no money, as you're not buying the property.

As you know, I was broke when I first got into real estate, sleeping on a couch with no income, until I got my first deal. Since I didn't even know what wholesaling was at the time, I made offers as a fix-and-flipper. So, my offers were incredibly low. Then, a REALTOR® whom I was working with to list offers on MLS properties said I could increase my price on some of the new properties because a landlord buyer would likely buy it from me rather than spend so much money on rehab. So, after nine months of calling agents and making offers, I finally got my first deal with this agent, and guess what? We did a wholesale. We found a buyer who wanted it for a rental. This gave me newfound confidence after having struggled to get a deal for nine months. Once I changed my offer strategy, we got a deal, and I didn't even need to rehab it. That was the confidence I needed to push even harder. Now I knew I could do it, and it was game on from there.

I'll wholesale five to fifteen properties each and every month across the country, but it isn't the only strategy out there. If you've ever seen me speak on stage, or if you've listened to my podcast, *The Science of Flipping*, you will know that I talk about how you need to be dynamic in how you go about finding the opportunity. You also want to be dynamic in how you exit. When I say dynamic, I mean to be diversified—don't just have one strategy; have at least two or three.

Fix and Flip

So, now you might be thinking you would rather fix and flip. Maybe you'd rather take a dumpster fire property that looks and smells terrible and turn it into a beautiful property, just like they do on TV. Well, that's an option, too, but this option has more risk. You actually need to buy the property, so you'll have to find the money to fund the deal. You don't need to personally have the money, but you'll likely want to raise it. Another risk you need to be aware of is the current state of the economy. Are interest rates going up or going down? Is there a lot of inventory or little inventory? What materials are being used in popular homes? Colors, styles, and what is trendy or currently fashionable can either make your property look fresh or make it seem outdated. Being a rehab flipper just involves more moving parts.

Now, I love rehab flipping. I've done well over six hundred of them. On the other hand, I also hate rehab flipping. I love it because there's something creative about turning what I like to call a dumpster fire property into a beautiful home for a family. The reason I hate rehabbing a property is, frankly, the contractors. There are good ones, of course, but even the good ones have their faults. Many times, they're way off on the budget or time frame. Both of those scenarios have cost me time and money, not to mention the risk factor. What if the appraisal comes in low, or the market shifts, and you can't get top dollar anymore? Did you build enough profit on the deal to handle those challenges?

As I write this, the interest rates have hit north of 7 percent for your typical mortgage. This has hurt a lot of buyers who can no longer afford the monthly mortgage payment. I just did a flip in northern Florida, and the interest rates were in the 5 percent range when I bought it. However, because my contractor faced some challenges and the city asked us to fix some things that we didn't account for, we went over both on time and budget. Now, on this deal, we had plenty of room to go over budget, but we didn't expect that we would need to hold the property for about nine months.

By the time it was set to list, interest rates were in the 7s, and our buyers offered much lower than the asking price because it was all they could afford. This home was in a first-time home-buyer neighborhood, so we were limited on potential buyers. All of these reasons led to us just breaking even on the deal after all the hard and private payments while holding the property for so long. I will tell you if you don't need to take on the risk, you can simply just wholesale the property, then just wholesale it. I love the ability to make money with little to no risk and then make decisions from there. Because if you become an expert marketer in finding the opportunity, then all the options become viable.

Buy and Hold

The buy-and-hold model has changed over time. Over the course of real estate sales, there have always been landlords, people who own the property, and people who lease it. I love the idea of owning real estate because you can increase the appreciation of the house just by natural market conditions, and you can add value that increases its worth. While wholesaling and rehabbing create active income (which is taxable), buying rental properties will create an opportunity for tax write-offs, so you will pay less taxes. There are many reasons for people to buy and hold a property.

The Biggest Mistake I Ever Made

Here is the biggest mistake I ever made. It isn't the seven figures I lost on the development I did. It isn't the quarter of a million dollars I lost on a multimillion-dollar flip. It's that I didn't buy rentals soon enough. And I don't want you all to make the same mistake. However, by no means am I saying you need to go buy a rental right now because, as I just mentioned, you will need the money, you will have to do the rehab, and you will have to deal with tenants. There are plenty of headaches that come along with being a landlord. And no, it is anything but passive. But the key to why it is so sexy is that not only can you make a monthly income, you can get tax write-offs, and you get to experience appreciation and equity. That is a "sexy" business model. I encourage you to start with the end in mind, decide what you want, decide who you need to be, commit, and take massive action. If you can start buying at least one rental property per year, within twenty years, you'll have a rental portfolio that will take care of you and your family for the rest of your life. All of this needs to start with a focus on finding the opportunity. And once you become great at finding salespeople, working with agents, and working with other investors to find those opportunities, you have options.

Let me tell you a story of a recent property I bought. It is a fourplex, and the fourplex needed a lot of work.

PRE PICS - 120 MICHAEL DONALD AVE, MOBILE, AL 366

We created value for the seller because they didn't have the money to do any renovation. So, they sold it to us at a discount because the property needed so much work. Well, we got it at a price that the property was lucrative—both as a long-term rental (because there are four units) or as a fix-and-flip. And because we are experts at finding these types of properties, we now have a choice on what we want to do for an exit. We can keep it and make thousands of dollars per month as a rental after we buy it, remodel it, and refinance it (part of the BRRRR method). As I'm writing this book, we're in the middle of remodeling it. We are expert marketers and understand how to find opportunities like this. Then, we created value for the seller to get the property at a deep enough price that it creates options. Now, we have the option to sell it off to another investor who likes to buy four-unit properties. That would make us multiple six figures. And that is the key to becoming a successful real estate investor. Do not be a one-trick pony. Do not only wholesale, or only rehab, or only buy rentals.

You should be doing it all.

Pro Tip: After 17 years of doing this business, one of the best tips I can give you is to NOT be a one-trick pony. You should be a utility belt. Depending on the best potential of the property, you might make different decisions on what you do with the property. The title of the book should say it all. *Flipping to Wealth.* There are times you should wholesale a property, fix and flip a property, and buy and hold a property. If you do this right, you will make a substantial income for yourself as well as build a massive portfolio.

Scan to Download All Resources to Find More Deals.
SCAN THE QR CODE:

CHAPTER SIX

Creative Finance Structure

"We cannot solve our problems with the same thinking we used when we created them."
– Albert Einstein

Creative financing is a really hot topic these days. This is, in part, because of some brilliant marketers and also because it is a strategically smart way to invest in real estate. So, from a thirty-thousand-foot perspective, creative financing is just that: *creative*. There are no hard and fast rules. If you can think of a strategy and a structure, then it likely will work. There are a few small rules you need to abide by, but for the most part, if it's an idea you can create, you can put it on paper, and as long as the seller is willing to do it, you can get the deal done.

Here's an example of a deal we just completed earlier this year. I personally called the owner of a two-unit complex in Cleveland, Ohio, because I wanted to teach my team how to make offers on creative financing. I asked the owner a few questions, including, "If I can get you more money, are you open to being flexible on the terms?" That one simple question opened the door for me to actually buy the property with 100 percent seller financing and little to no money out-of-pocket except for closing costs.

He answered: "Well, tell me more. What do you mean?"

Then I asked the following questions:

- How large is the loan you have on the property?
- What are your payments every month?
- What are your typical rents like?

Since the owner was already an investor and the property was a duplex with no mortgage, I concluded that this was a perfect property for a creative finance structure, with the seller holding the mortgage and becoming the bank. Duplexes are typically an investment-type property, so there were no actual monthly payments besides maintenance, repairs, taxes, and insurance. This property could rent somewhere in the mid to high teens every month between $1,600 and $1,900.

The next question I asked the seller was, "Why would you be interested in selling now?" He said it was because there was only one tenant occupying the duplex and one unit was open, so it could be a good time for him to sell the property, take his profits, and move on to another investment property. (For a complete list of Questions to Ask Sellers, scan the QR code at the end of this chapter.)

It's important to note that the seller just told me he wanted to buy another investment property. Now I know he's essentially going to take his profits and reinvest them into a future investment property. So, what if, by being creative, I could simply show him that he could actually keep his money in play and earn a higher return on investment by being the bank rather than being the landlord?

So, based on the increased purchase value and because he was acting as the bank, I could pay more on the purchase price, and his return on his investment would actually increase. At the same time, he wouldn't have the headaches that come with being a landlord. All that was needed was to occupy the vacant unit and do all the repairs. So, at the end of this conversation, we both realized this was going to be a win-win. He had to think about it for a day or two and quickly got back to me, saying he was good to go to finance 100 percent of this purchase as the bank, as long as I came in and took on all the repairs once I owned it.

So, the seller actually converted over to the bank. I became the owner, so all the ownership responsibilities now landed on me, and all I had to do was pay him principal plus interest, which was negotiated to be 5 percent. Now, this is a creative finance deal.

A popular form of creative financing is "subject to," which means you simply leave the current bank loan in place with the original borrower's name on the loan while the new owner pays the bank mortgage. Now, there is a fine line that you will need to walk, as there is a "due on sale clause," which is typical when working with banks. However, I've found in my time of doing hundreds of "subject to" deals that as long as the mortgage is being paid on time and as long as you're making payments regularly, you will almost never experience a bank calling the loan due.

The structure of "subject to" deals has many layers because you can execute what is known as a "wrap deal." In this arrangement, the existing loan remains in place, but through negotiations with the seller, they use the equity they have in the home to create a new loan, which they then extend to you.

Here is a simple example. Say you want to buy a property for $150,000, and the seller has a $100,000 loan but is also willing to turn $50,000 of their equity into a loan. They essentially become the bank for that $50,000 and lend it to you. Now, there is no money that is actually exchanged; it is just paperwork. As the buyer, you will essentially have two loans—one with the bank and one with the seller. The interest rate you negotiate with a seller is exactly that: *negotiable*. However, the interest rate with the bank is not. You will essentially just take over whatever payments were based on the loan that the previous seller received.

For the sake of this example, we didn't negotiate any money down to the seller. In this case, you would need to come to the closing table essentially with closing costs to close the deal. Again, a $100,000 bank loan, a $50,000 loan to the previous owner at, let's say, another 5 percent, you close the deal at a $150,000 purchase price, and you pay both lenders separately.

Now, there are many different versions of creative finance deals, such as **novations**. Novations are a subject that has been increasingly talked about in recent years. The structure is essentially making an offer to the seller, which gives us an opportunity to find a buyer as a wholesaler from the MLS. A novation has very specific paperwork. The paperwork gets signed off by the seller, which allows us, as the buyer, to list the property and market it anywhere we feel it fits. That paperwork is written in a way that makes it completely legal to take over the sale of that property. The paperwork is an **attorney-in-fact**, and it's an important document that you want the seller to sign off on to give you the ability to list this property. More often than not, you won't need to buy the property. You won't need to rehab it. You're essentially finding a buyer through the MLS and wholesaling the property. In this situation, you could do a double close, which I talked about in previous chapters, or you could simply assign the contract to your buyer. Both can happen on a novation.

The definition of novation has changed over time. Here is the old-school way of explaining a novation. Many years ago, we would talk to a seller who wanted a number that we couldn't get to with a cash offer. But we realized if we could rehab the home, there would be profits. So, we negotiated with the seller on a number we would spend to remodel the home. Then, we would put a **lien** against the property, and once we sold, they would get the money we agreed upon, and we would take our profits as well as the money we put into the rehab.

Since then, however, it has become more common to use an attorney-in-fact to list the property on the MLS.

A common question we get is: "Why would a seller sell you a home creatively rather than just listing it with a REALTOR® on the MLS (multiple listing service)."

First of all, some sellers don't need to sell; they're interested in selling in order to get the top dollar. Others realize that if they sell their investment property right now, they will take a big profit, which will then be taxed. They don't want to take on that tax liability, so they structure a creative finance deal with us so that the taxable end is stretched out for a long time.

Other sellers might be in desperation; they might know that, very shortly, they won't be able to afford the mortgage payments, which will result in them losing their home, and they need a resolution now. Remember, the more value you provide to the seller, the higher chance you will get the deal.

Creative financing creates a great opportunity to build a rental portfolio for investors looking to buy investments without going to banks to get a loan. It creates an opportunity to buy a rental property that is already performing without needing to come in with a lot of your own cash. Remember, you don't need your own money to buy rentals or to fix and flip.

Sometimes, it's as simple as getting creative, where you don't need any money at all. This has helped me accumulate millions of dollars in rental properties while also offering a structure to the sellers so they see the value I'm offering. In doing this, I'm able to build my wealth through my rental portfolio. In fact, not only do I do it myself, but I teach other people how to creatively structure wholesale deals, flips, and rentals. And I teach people to build their wealth in a creative manner.

I want you to understand the structure of a creative finance deal. I want you to understand how creative you can be. I want you to understand that there really is no bad idea when creating or structuring a creative finance offer. I was taught this many moons ago by one of my mentors. He let me know that as long as I can put an idea down on paper and as long as the seller agrees to it, there is no bad idea. And while this mentor told me this many years ago, it still remains true.

I want this for all of you who are reading this book.

Pro Tip: Creative Financing "creates the opportunity."

There is no one-size-fits-all solution, and the more creative you can be in solving the homeowner's problem, the more deals you will close.

You can become a deal architect and put deals together that few will know how to do.

Most investors these days are simply "wholesalers," but if you refine your skills in creative financing, the sky's the limit for you.

For a Complete List of *Questions to Ask Sellers*.
SCAN THE QR CODE:

CHAPTER SEVEN

The BRRR method

"Success is not final, failure is not fatal: It is the courage to continue that counts."
– Winston Churchill

You need to buy rentals, and you need to buy rentals *now*. As I mentioned previously, my biggest mistakes were not the missed flips, where I lost money, or the development play, where I lost a *whole lot* of money. My biggest mistake was that from day one, I didn't have my eyes set on building wealth through buying properties for my rental portfolio. So, in recent years, I have started to do that. I don't want you to make the same mistake I did. Here's a disclaimer: If you have a W-2 job and you have, say, $45,000 saved up, I'm not necessarily advising you to spend that money on one rental because you read this book, and then you're done. You're tapped out. In this chapter, I'll tell you how you can still buy a rental without needing to use your own money. To be fair, I understand that I previously spoke about focusing on wholesaling if you have a W-2, and that's because the science of wholesaling is actually marketing and lead generation. If you generate enough leads, you'll be able to cherry-pick one rental per year (or more) to buy—without needing to use any of your own money.

The example I'm going to give you is from the "BRRRR" method (Buy it, Rehab it, Rent it, Refinance, Repeat). I myself use this method, and I teach about this method to thousands of the Science of Flipping community members.

Here is the structure of this method. First, you need to find a deal, and then you're going to need money to fund it. A lot of companies out there are called hard money lenders, which means their interest rates tend to be much higher than the banks—as high as 18 percent.

Some of you may think you will never use a hard money lender. However, a reason why you should use one is to acquire the property. It isn't a long-term loan, and you're not terribly invested in this interest rate. It's meant to be a bridge or a Band-Aid to get it to the point of refinancing out with a long-term loan with a much better interest rate. On these deals, hard money lenders will typically fund somewhere between 75 and 90 percent of your acquisition. They also, for the most part, will reimburse you for your rehab budget.

Let me tell you a quick story about leverage and why I believe in it so much. I was watching an interview with Grant Cardone and "Hospitality King" Dave Grutman. Dave Grutman has ten of the top restaurants in Miami and multiple nightclubs, and he just opened two restaurants and a nightclub in Vegas. The interview was about how Dave Grutman scaled his restaurant business early on. His answer was that he took on a capital partner. He brought in a lot of money with debt and equity to get further and faster. He realized he could have 100 percent of one restaurant or, at this point, a smaller percentage of a billion-dollar enterprise. I hope this helps you realize that even when it comes to one property, good debt, and equity partners are beneficial.

So, let me give you an example. If you're buying a property for $100,000 and you need $50,000 for a rehab budget, the hard money lender will give you somewhere between $75,000 and $90,000 on your purchase price, and they will reimburse you for the $50,000 that you put into the rehab. Now, I advise all people who are rehabbing to pay their construction crew in 25 percent increments. So, if the rehab is $50,000, you'll essentially want to pay them $12,500 per payment until it is done. This allows the hard money lender to reimburse you for the $12,500 that you initially gave the contractor, so you're always turning over only $12,500 and not $50,000 in one chunk. Now, you will still need to bring anywhere from $10 to $25,000 to the purchase, plus the $12,500 for the initial draw to the contractor. Let's say you're going to need to bring $35,000 to the deal.

So, in this example, you have a savings of $60,000. So, you technically could use your own money, and at some point, it may not be a bad idea. But let me walk you through what I teach to all of my Science of Flipping community members: How and why to use other people's money. Something as simple as a cash advance from a credit card company can be utilized for $35,000. You also can go to your friends and family and ask for a loan or bring them in on the property and give them equity because you've borrowed their money.

I also encourage you to talk to people who have retirement accounts, which typically don't make any money for them. If they're not investing or getting at least a 10 percent return on their money, then they're actually losing money.

Some of my readers might be thinking, *My friends and family don't come from money. We don't have money.* But maybe what you fail to realize is that some of these retirement plans can actually be the money they can utilize as a loan to you so you can buy this property, and they can get at least 10 percent interest from you or potentially be an equity partner on the asset. Both work.

Now, if you've never raised money or had these discussions, it can feel a little intimidating. I understand that. But as I teach all of my Science of Flipping members, it's actually a lot simpler than you would think. In fact, people usually wait for these opportunities but aren't aware of them. So, if you simply voice that you have an opportunity for them to make an investment and get a return or get equity, they will actually start jumping on board.

As recently as this week, as I write this book, I made an offer on my social media that there's an investment opportunity on a very large property in Houston, Texas. It was shared only on social media, and I have privately received text messages from many friends and family members who are interested in learning more, as they would like to be part of that investment.

The key here is that I only told people about the opportunity, and now I'm privately receiving text messages from people who are on my phone, and I'm receiving DMs for those who are following me through social media. There's a lot of interest out there—it's just that you aren't asking for what you're looking for.

Now, let's get back to the deal. Once you're finished with the rehab, you can go find a tenant. Now, I know you're probably busy with work, kids, and life in general. So, I always advise you to use a property manager. They typically charge a fee between 8 and 10 percent, so you need to ensure the property achieves the rent you expect. At the end of the day, you need to make sure it's a profitable purchase each month. Once it's rented, you can approach a bank, which will refinance up to 85 percent of the new appraised value, also known as the "after repair value" (ARV). Banks will lend up to 85 percent of that new value.

So, as long as you bought the property right (at numbers low enough to make it a deal), you added value through the remodel, and the tenant is paying market rent, the bank feels comfortable about financing you rather aggressively. At that point, the bank should be able to refinance nearly 100 percent of your money from the deal. In some instances, the bank will actually do a **cash-out refinance**, which happens when you create so much value that up to 80 percent of the value is more than the money you have invested into the property. There is massive value in building your rental portfolio.

The structure of the BRRRR method is my preferred strategy, and I coach all of the Science of Flipping community members in using it.

I encourage you to use this method as you go down the path of being a dynamic real estate investor who is not only making a lot of money wholesaling and flipping, but also buying and holding.

Pro Tip: Many people initially tell me that they don't have much money or don't come from wealth. However, that is completely irrelevant when it comes to real estate. It is the secret of using other people's money (OPM) that will allow you to buy these deals. You can amass a massive rental portfolio with none of your own money as long as you know where to find the money.

Buy More Rentals With These Resources.
SCAN THE QR CODE:

CHAPTER EIGHT

Raising Private Money Isn't Hard

"Life is really simple, but we insist on making it complicated."
– Confucius

Now, you may be wondering, "How do I not use my own money when rehabbing deals or buying rentals?" This brings us to raising private money. The U.S. Securities and Exchange Commission (SEC) has some very specific rules about raising private money that you don't want to infringe on because it's against the law. The SEC closely watches whether you're guaranteeing returns and soliciting investments from the public. However, there is a way around that, which is by starting a **private placement memorandum** (PPM). This would allow you to guarantee a return to your investors.

Raising private capital is doable and can become easy after you get the hang of it. It really is about what opportunity you're offering your investor. I do it all the time in my business, and I teach all the Science of Flipping community members how to do it. I give my community members a couple of different simple scripts that they can use to help them raise money. They do it privately and don't make any guarantees.

They show the opportunity as something people can make a decision on whether they want to lend or even become a capital partner.

As I mentioned in the previous chapter, a retirement account can be transferred into a self-directed account. Once that happens, the owner of that account can now lend. However, they can't use their money themselves for a loan; they need to lend it to another person or entity. Now, if you know there are trillions of dollars—you heard me right—in retirement accounts across the nation, then you know there are a lot of people who have money just sitting around.

You might be reading this and thinking, *I don't have money in my savings account or checking account, but I have $100,000 in a retirement account.* You might even be thinking, *I could be a lender on someone else's deal.* And the same is true for millions of other people across the country. You just need to give them the opportunity to become a lender. The best way I can tell you how to do that is to let them know you're looking to borrow money for real estate.

Now, how could you potentially do that? Well, you can do it over a cup of coffee, through social media, in group meetings, or you can go to Real Estate Investors Association (REIA) meetings. The key here is to let people know you're looking. Most people overcomplicate this, as they believe people will be sensitive about money conversations. But you're trying to help people make more money, and everyone likes making more money. Now, you *do* want to be respectable, and you absolutely *don't* want to make this sound like a "get-rich-quick" scheme. However, you do want to provide them with the knowledge that there are real estate investment opportunities that could be good options for them to partake in as an investor. Would they be open? The key is to tell them about opportunities rather than ask them for money. Many of my private money lenders love being a part of the deal because they get to be part of an industry they find interesting. You're giving people the opportunity to be a part of that world without needing to deal with the headaches of finding the property, doing the construction, dealing with the contractors, trying to sell the property, or trying to find a tenant. Frankly, some are okay with making 8 percent or more on their money. Others might be more fired up to be one of your equity partners.

Now you understand there is an actual process to raise private money and, in the same way, there is a process to find the deal. You also need to define your intentions and then take action toward those intentions. So, if you intend to raise $100,000 by the end of reading this book, you need to put that intention out into the universe. You need to be talking about it. You don't need to promise or guarantee people anything, but you need to talk about your interest in raising money for some real estate opportunities that you're looking at. I'm telling you now that you will be shocked to know how many people will be interested. Everyone loves real estate. Everyone loves making money. And everyone loves paying the IRS less taxes, which real estate can help you and others achieve.

An example of that is the large apartment complex I'm working on in Houston, Texas. The reason that deal makes so much sense, and why I'm raising money for it, in part, is so I can avoid paying the IRS taxes on my income. That's one reason why raising capital for this deal is important. I also, obviously, like the income that the deal would kick-off to me. And I like the fact that there's appreciation involved that I'll experience on my own. Even if you're buying a single-family home, all three of those are true. You can bring in an equity partner instead of just a lender. For example, if your aunt Susan has a $100,000 retirement account and says, "Hey, little Freddie, I would be interested in doing a deal with you and bringing money to this deal as a partnership, not as a lender." Well, you and your aunt Susan will be able to take part in the depreciation of the asset, which gives you a tax write-off. You will be able to take part in a monthly income, and you'll be able to take part in appreciation, too. This means when you guys decide to sell it, there's a whole lot more money in there than when you started because the home, apartment, duplex, triplex, or quadplex has increased in value.

So, now you know it's important that you understand how to raise private money and what to say. But the most important part of raising money is making sure there is a deal to use it on.

Pro Tip: There are three places to find private money.

1. Inner Circle - This is your closest friends and family.

2. Outer Circle - This is your work friends or gym friends. The people you might grab a burger with but probably won't be invited to Christmas dinner.

3. Social Circle - This is exactly what you are thinking. It is all your "friends" on social media.

Now, you might be saying to yourself that you don't like social media or that you don't have a lot of friends on social media. That's okay. Just make sure you are using social media. It works.

Raise More Money With These Scripts.
SCAN THE QR CODE:

BONUS CHAPTER

Social Media

As I wrap up my final edits to this book, I want to include a short chapter on the power of social media. I know some of you might be hesitant at this point, but please bear with me.

If you're not using social media for branding purposes, you're missing out. Remember, people want to do business with those they know, like, and trust. If they don't know what you do, how you do it, or what you're looking for, they're unlikely to do business with you.

I understand that social media can often seem like just dancing videos and pictures of what people are eating for dinner, but that's not how I suggest you use it.

I encourage you to build a brand around yourself. It's really not as hard as you might think. There's a three-point strategy I use, and it has created a personal brand that people are naturally drawn to.

1. Let people know who you are.

You can do this by simply posting some of your thoughts, motivational quotes, images of your family, images of a deal you bought, etc. Try not to get into religion or politics.

2. Let people know what you do.

You can show yourself walking properties. You can post about the newest deal you bought. You can write a comment about looking for more investment deals, etc. It is simple and effective.

3. Let people know what you're looking for.

When you're looking to raise money for deals or even find more opportunities, just make a post about it. Don't overcomplicate things; a simple post will do.

For example: "Looking to buy my next rental property, does anyone know of an opportunity?"

The key to social media is to use it—not for posting about your meals, but for business and building your brand. You don't need to be a famous social media influencer, but if used correctly, social media can significantly accelerate your journey to financial freedom.

Don't be afraid! Most people are hesitant to post because they're afraid of criticism. Don't be that person—just go for it. It will speed up the entire process for you.

CONCLUSION
You Can Do This. I Believe in You

"Decide what you want, commit to it, take massive action, fail, be resilient and keep going."
– Justin Colby

If you have read this far, then now is the time for you to get into real estate and play it all out. Whether it's part-time or full-time, real estate is the only vehicle that can help you earn massive amounts of income and, at the same time, accumulate incredible amounts of wealth. You know, I've been around long enough to know that the days are long, but the years are short. Time is not on our side. We need to make the most of it. So, this is not a book for the future. This is a book for *now*. You need to get in the game *now*. And be patient with your expectations of results. If you remember the fifth pillar of success—remove your time expectation on results—then you will keep your head down and do the necessary work to make a lot of income wholesaling and flipping, and at the same time, building a lot of wealth.

Let's take Warren Buffett, for example. Warren Buffett is, in large part, known as the smartest investor of our times. But let's look at how quickly he earned that title. At age twenty-one, his net worth was

$20,000. He made his first million at the age of fifty-six. It took him thirteen years to become a millionaire, and it took him thirty-five years to become a billionaire. The game of real estate is the only one I know where someone with my skill set—who may not be the sharpest tool in the shed—can become a millionaire through *income* and a billionaire through *assets*. We aren't all as smart as Warren Buffett, but if you can have just a slice of his patience, just a piece of his fortitude, you too can make it big.

You see, I believe in something called the "CIA." No, I'm not talking about the government agency. I'm talking about "commitment, intention, and action." The "CIA" has served me well. I committed to being a successful real estate investor. I aligned my intentions to do so. And with that, I moved forward by taking massive actions. You see, if your actions align with your intentions and you're deeply committed, anything is achievable. For those who want it bad enough, for those who are connected to it enough, you can quit your job. You, too, can become a millionaire. And you, too, can become a billionaire through real estate. You just have to get started. Some of you who are reading this book may already be in the game. You might already be wholesaling or flipping, or maybe you've accumulated a couple of rentals.

And for those of you who are okay with having a handful of rentals, and that's as far as you want to take it, it's all good. I'm glad you enjoyed the book. I hope you share it with others. But for the reader like me, who knows real estate is their path, who knows that they're making a decision about who they need to be to become a millionaire and then a multi-millionaire through real estate, then I would tell you to read this book again.

This book is the blueprint to *Flipping to Wealth*. It's great to make a lot of money flipping homes, but what's even better is creating a lifestyle where you have the time and freedom to do *what* you want *when* you want. You can do this by creating income that comes in each and every month, whether you're working or not. I want to repeat the Five Pillars of Success one more time for you all, as I firmly believe that if you ingrain these into yourself, you will actually become successful.

1. **Decide what you want, and decide who you need to be to get it.**
2. **Commit.**
3. **Take massive action.**
4. **Become extremely uncomfortable.**
5. **Remove your time expectation on results.**

Now, all five of these are incredibly important for success. But if you put all five together, the real estate game is *fun*. Is there a risk? Sure. But with risk comes reward. Is it easy? No, but it is simple. This is *not* rocket science. You don't need to get your master's or PhD. You need to have a work ethic and follow a proven path.

Let me help you understand my philosophy on life. Every minute you play small, live a mediocre life, and are okay with being good enough, *you're wasting your life*. We only get one of these things called life. There is no practice. You deserve an incredible, amazing, spectacular life, and it's up to you to create that.

The nice part about real estate is that it's pretty straightforward. It's really all math. If the numbers work, then it's a deal, and you have reduced your downside risk.

The fear that creeps up in your mind is all regarding failure. So, like I said, if the numbers work, it's really hard to fail. Don't get too caught up on the risk as it is calculated.

Take what you can from this book and accumulate as many rentals as you can throughout the years for as long as you can. I'll tell you that I personally will never quit real estate. From my first deal in 2007 to this very moment—as I'm about to close on my very first 550-door apartment complex in Houston—I know I will forever be in real estate as a real estate investor. The markets may change, the game may change, the rules may change, and the economy may change, but I will stay steadfast and focused, and I hope that you will, too. Now, if you can do me a favor, please share this book with as many people as possible. Buy it as presents for holidays and for birthdays. Help people understand the process not just to make incredible income and flip properties but to build a massive net worth by holding them.

I hope to see you all soon.

Don't Miss All the Social Media Resources Here.
SCAN THE QR CODE:

Terminology

1031 exchange: Allows real estate investors to swap one investment property for another and defer capital gains taxes, but only if IRS rules are met.

After repair value (ARV): The value of a property after repairs and improvements have been made.

Appreciation: The increase in the value of a property over time.

Assignment contract: A wholesale strategy used by investors to facilitate the sale of a property between an owner and a buyer.

Attorney-in-fact: A document designating someone to act on behalf of another, similar to a power of attorney.

Bird dog: A bird dog is a person who looks for motivated sellers and undervalued properties to pass on to a real estate investor in exchange for a fee.

BRRRR method: A real estate investing strategy. BRRRR is an acronym for buy, rehab, rent, refinance, repeat. Using this method, investors purchase properties that need renovations. They rehab them and rent them out. Then, after they've built up equity, they do a cash-out refinance to use their profit on another property.

Buy and hold: A long-term investment strategy where an investor purchases a property and holds on to it for an extended period of time.

Buy box: A list of criteria determined by an investor that a property must meet to qualify for purchase.

Buyers list: Active investors who buy fix-and-flips or rentals. This information can be found easily on data platforms.

Cash flow: The net income generated by a rental property, after all other costs and expenses have been accounted for and subtracted from gross rents.

Cash-out refinance: A mortgage refinancing option that enables borrowers to increase their loan amount, leveraging their home equity to access cash.

Closing costs: Fees and expenses paid at the end of a real estate transaction. They include charges like appraisal fees, title insurance, and attorney fees.

Closing docs: Documents from title and escrow that need your signature to close the transaction.

Contract assignment: An assignable contract that has a provision allowing the holder to give away the obligations and rights of the contract to another party or person before the contract's expiration date.

Creative financing: Involves non-traditional methods to fund property purchases, such as seller financing, lease options, and partnerships, providing flexibility beyond conventional bank loans.

Depreciation: The expense of a fixed asset over its useful life. Fixed assets are tangible objects acquired by a business.

Distressed property: A property in poor condition or under financial distress (such as foreclosure or short sale), often sold below market value.

Double close: Also referred to as a back-to-back closing, a double closing is when a wholesaler purchases a property and immediately resells it to an end buyer. There are two separate escrow numbers, and the wholesaler takes the title to the house even just for a short amount of time.

Equity: Typically refers to shareholders' equity, which represents the residual value to shareholders after debts and liabilities have been settled.

Escrow: Escrow is the arrangement of one company holding and managing the payment of funds required for two parties in a given transaction

Fixing and flipping: The strategy of purchasing a property, making improvements to it, and then putting it back on the market for a profit.

Foreclosure: The legal process by which a lender attempts to recover the amount owed on a defaulted loan by taking ownership of the mortgaged property and selling it. Typically, default is triggered when a borrower misses a specific number of monthly payments, but it can also happen when the borrower fails to meet other terms in the mortgage document.

Hard money loan: A short-term loan based chiefly on the value of the property used as collateral and not the creditworthiness of the buyer.

Land lease: A clause in a real estate contract that grants the renter or lessee the right, but not the obligation, to extend his or her use of a property beyond the term specified in the contract.

Lien: A public record of a legal claim placed against the property because of an unpaid debt.

Motivated sellers: Homeowners who typically have a financial motivation to sell. Although it is not always financial, you might come across various other forms of motivation. Motivation allows investors the best ability to negotiate a favorable purchase price.

Multiple listing service (MLS): Databases that are created, maintained and paid for by real estate professionals to help their clients and other REALTORS® buy and sell property.

Novation: Replacing someone or something in a contract with someone or something else.

Over-leverage: When a business has borrowed too much money and is unable to make payments on interest, principal or maintenance.

Pocket listings: These are off-market listings that are marketed to buyers privately and are not listed on the MLS.

Private placement memorandum (PPM): Sometimes called an offering document, it's a legal document provided to prospective investors or buyers.

Property management: Companies that manage all operations of the rental property, such as selecting tenants, collecting rents and deposits, handling maintenance issues, and even responding to tenant disputes or complaints.

Real estate auction: Once homes are foreclosed on or seized, they are listed as auctions and scheduled. You will have to register and submit a refundable deposit of 5–10 percent of the property's expected selling price to the entity holding the auction.

Real estate brokerage: The company that covers individual real estate agents, making sure that all transactions are legal and compliant.

Realtor: A licensed professional who represents buyers or sellers in real estate transactions.

Skip trace: Using a software to take an address or a person's name and find out their contact information.

Short sale: An asking price for a home that is less than the amount that is due on its existing mortgage.

Title: The title company insures the property's title with policies to the buyer and the lender to protect against problems with the property or the title

Turnkey property: A property in residential real estate that, upon purchase, can be rented out immediately by the buyer.

Underwriting: Analyzing the property to make sure it's a profitable deal

Vacancy rate: The percentage of all available units in a rental property, such as a hotel or apartment complex, that are vacant or unoccupied at a particular time.

Wholesaling: When an investor agrees to buy a property and then quickly sells the contract to another buyer at a higher price.

Sources: https://www.investopedia.com/

https://arabellacapital.com/glossary-of-real-estate-investing-terms

THANK YOU FOR READING MY BOOK!

DOWNLOAD YOUR FREE GIFTS

Just to say thanks for buying and reading my book, I put together some bonus resources for you. Enjoy! would

Scan the QR Code:

I appreciate your interest in my book and value your feedback as it helps me improve future versions of this book. I would appreciate it if you could leave your invaluable review on Amazon.com with your feedback. Thank you!

Made in the USA
Columbia, SC
22 December 2024